FRANCE COLORING BOOK

Charming 19th Century France

FREDERIC DURAND

Printed in the United States of America
ISBN: 978-1619495326

CONTENTS

This page intentionally left blank.

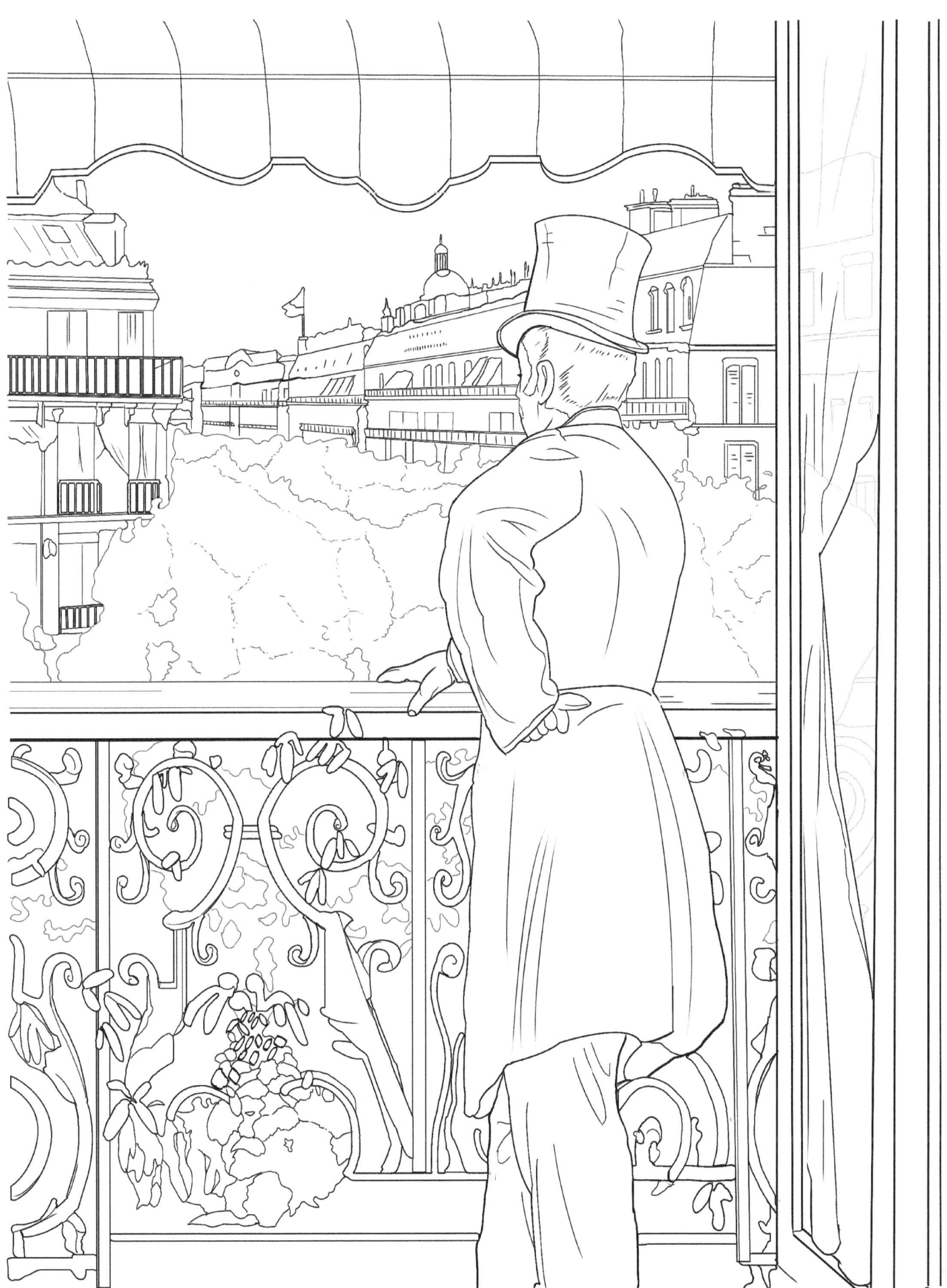

3

Plate 1.
A Man at the Balcony, Boulevard Haussmann, 1880.

Caillebotte painted different versions of the *Homme au balcon*. The original perspective and the vanishing point catches the viewer's eye directing the gaze outside to the Haussmann Paris. Here we witness again the recurring theme of windows and balconies favored by the artist. The protagonist in a top hat and a fashionable upper-class suit is immersed in the grandiosity of the exterior space. Outside we can witness the tree lined Haussmann Boulevard and the modern vast space that has opened up after the reconstruction of Paris. Haussmann Paris, a modern city plan that is modeled on a symmetrical and geometrical grid, dividing the medieval scattered Paris into neatly planned arrondissements and districts, is also one of the favorite and recurring scenes in Caillebotte's paintings.

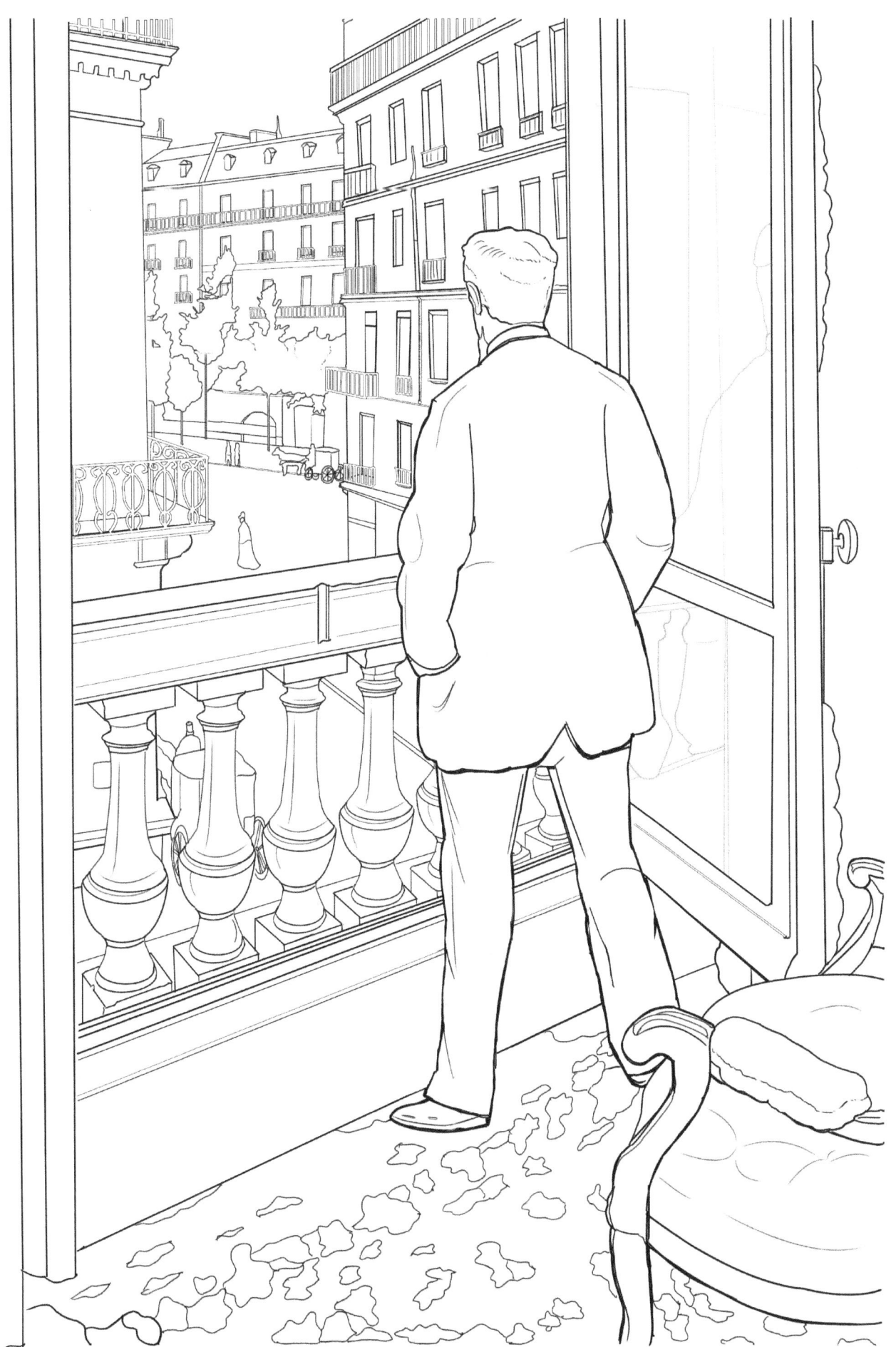

Plate 2.
Young Man At His Window, **1875.**

Caillebotte painted different versions of the *Homme au balcon*. The original perspective and the vanishing point catches the viewer's eye directing the gaze outside to the Haussmann Paris. Here we witness again the recurring theme of windows and balconies favored by the artist. The protagonist in a top hat and a fashionable upper-class suit is immersed in the grandiosity of the exterior space. Outside we can witness the tree lined Haussmann Boulevard and the modern vast space that has opened up after the reconstruction of Paris. Haussmann Paris, a modern city plan that is modeled on a symmetrical and geometrical grid, dividing the medieval scattered Paris into neatly planned arrondissements and districts, is also one of the favorite and recurring scenes in Caillebotte's paintings.

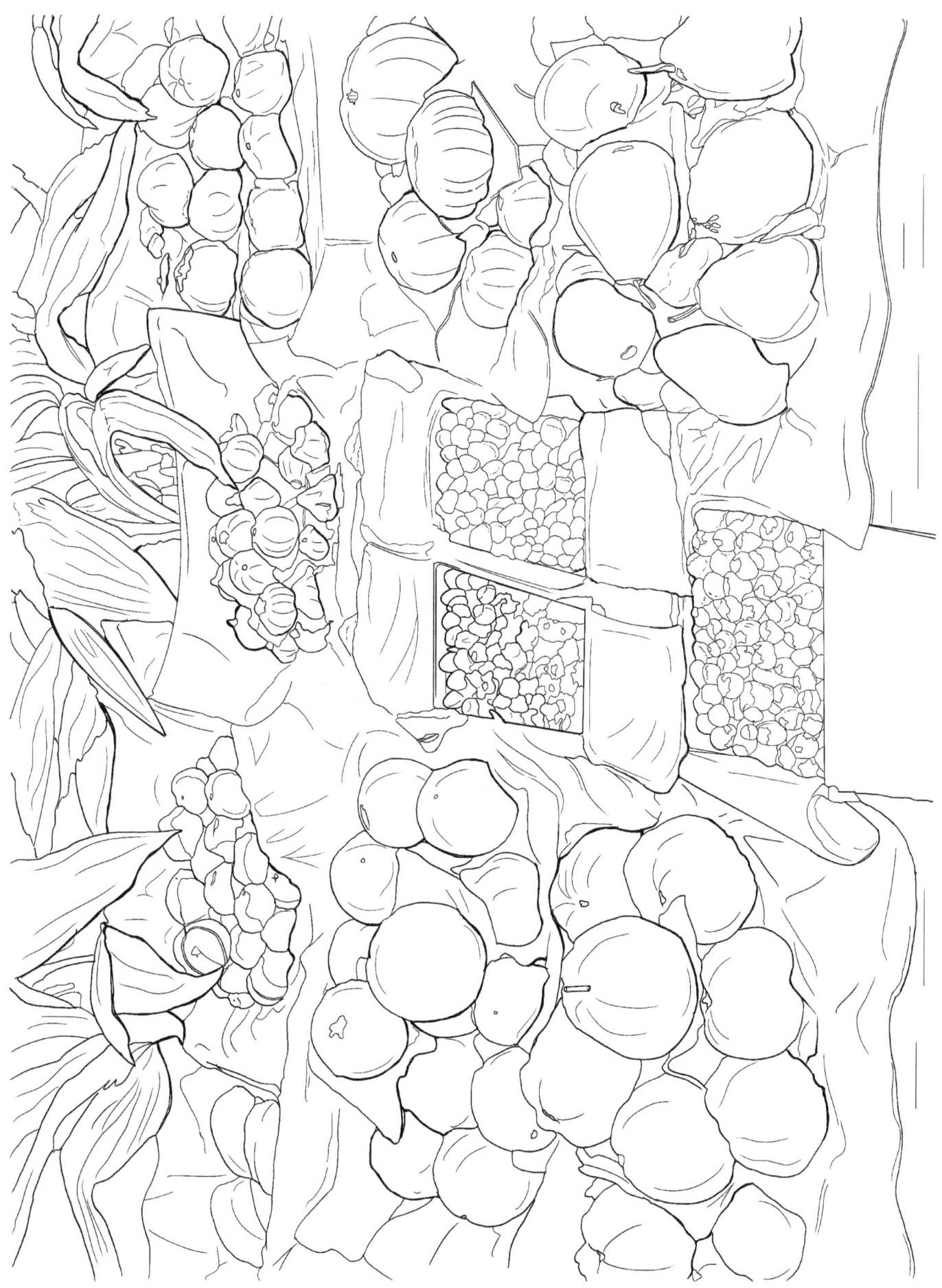

Plate 3.
Fruits Displayed on a Stand

This painting belongs to important still life compositions executed for the main part between 1881-1882. The close-up view of seasonal fruits stacked up on a market display are painted with great attention to detail and to the reflection of light, creating bold patterns of bright and vivid colors. The painter depicts the fruits as if they were cushioned sparkling colored gemstones on a vendor's stand. The sensual brushstrokes suggest the juiciness and ripeness of the fruits. This painting is reminiscent of the fruit and flower gardens of the painter as well as his passion for the horticulture. The work was destined to decorate a dining room of the artist's friend Monsieur Albert Courtier, a notary in Meaux.

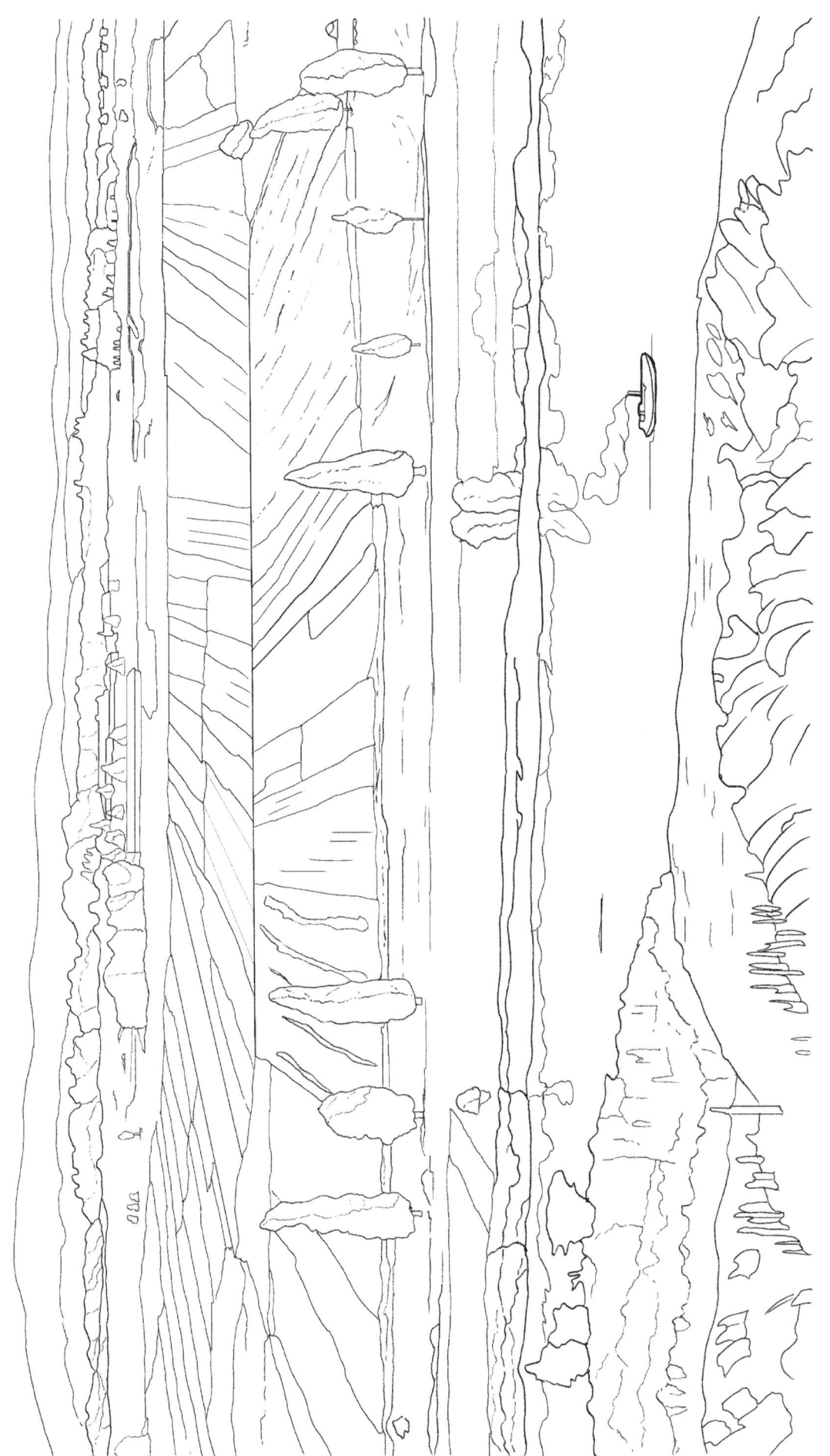

Plate 4.
The Plane of Gennevilliers

This painting belongs to important still life compositions executed for the main part between 1881-1882. The close-up view of seasonal fruits stacked up on a market display are painted with great attention to detail and to the reflection of light, creating bold patterns of bright and vivid colors. The painter depicts the fruits as if they were cushioned sparkling colored gemstones on a vendor's stand. The sensual brushstrokes suggest the juiciness and ripeness of the fruits. This painting is reminiscent of the fruit and flower gardens of the painter as well as his passion for the horticulture. The work was destined to decorate a dining room of the artist's friend Monsieur Albert Courtier, a notary in Meaux.

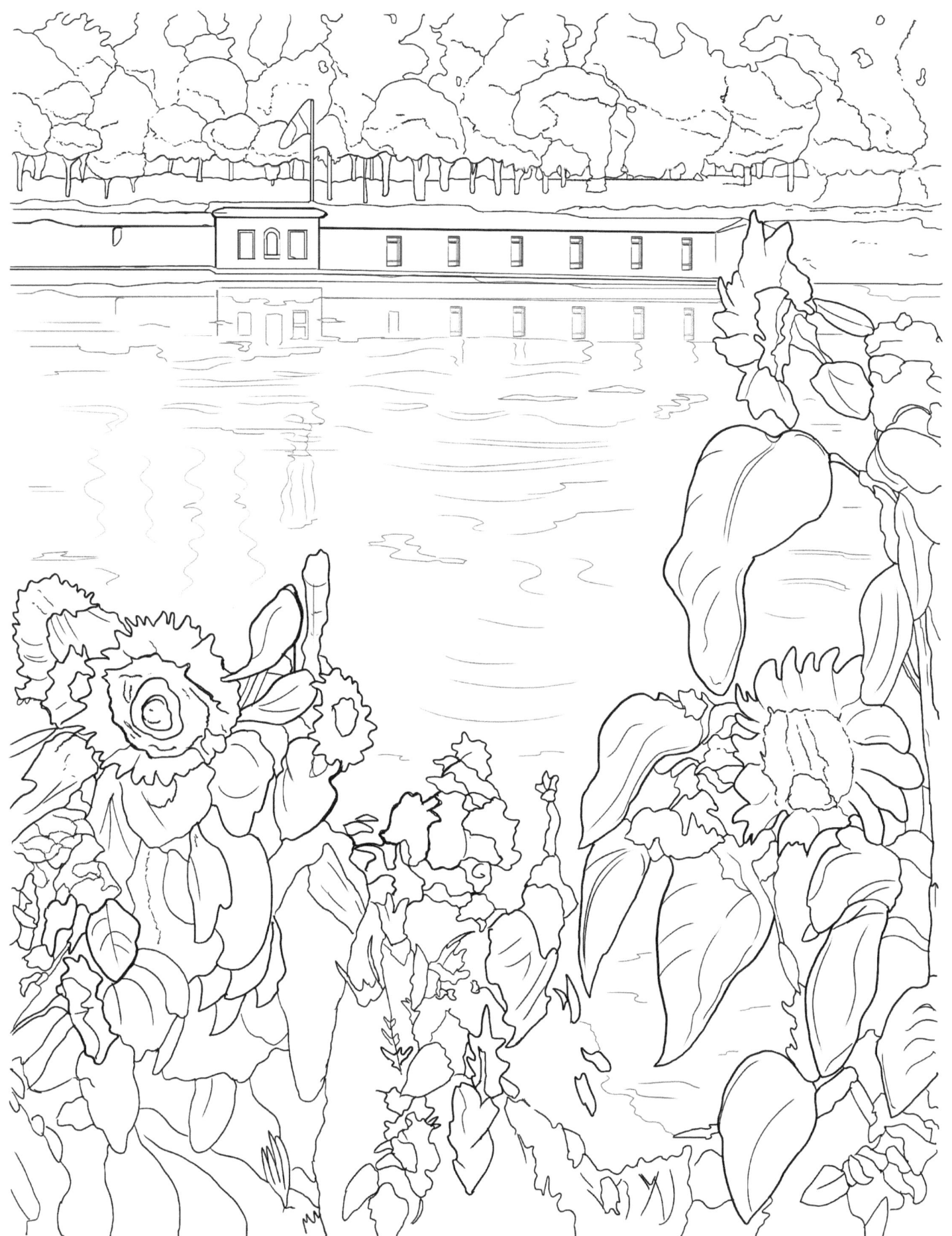

Plate 5.
Sunflowers on the Banks of the Seine

The painting depicts cheerful brightly colored sunflowers in front of a river bank. The lush and vivid sunflower heads are protagonists of this canvas, painted in thickly sensuous brushstrokes. In the background a white barge or a boat house is reflected in the water by vast horizontal brushstrokes. The tricolored French flag produces an elongated beautiful reflection in the water, along with the reflections of the green foliage and bright sunlight. The brushstrokes are dynamic and full of life. Again, as we have witnessed in Caillebotte's other landscapes, despite the non present moving human figures, the artist's swift and elongated brushstrokes and thick layers of paint are capable to animate the painting with movement and motion, creating a sense of human presence.

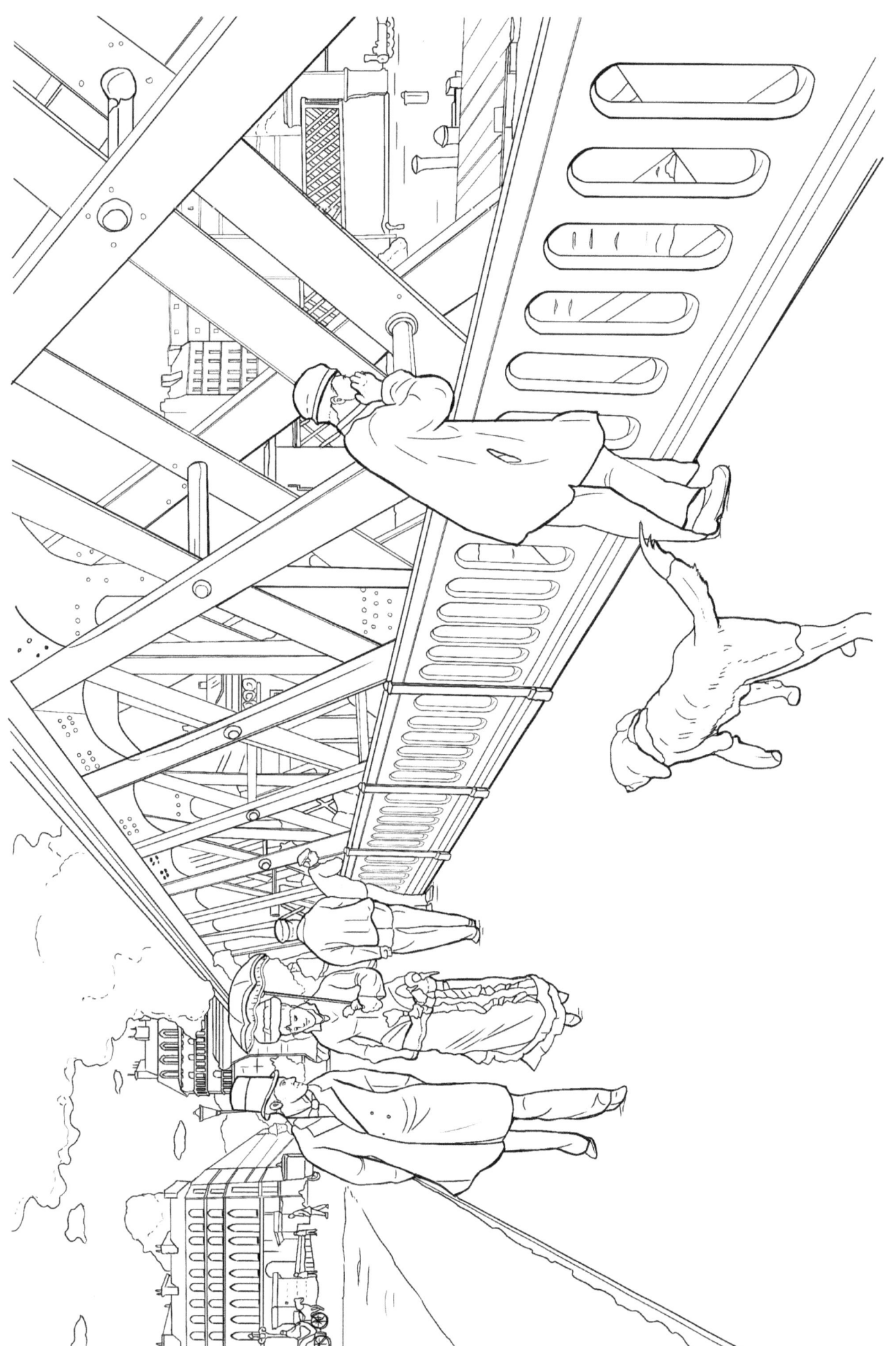

Plate 6.
The Europe Bridge (Le Pont de l'Europe), 1876.

With the development and popularity of the railroad lines in the 19th century, the train stations started playing an important part in everyday city life. The Saint-Lazare train station was one of those modern Parisian city life spaces that have inspired many impressionists, such as Monet, by its trains submerged in steam and the atmospheric movement in the stations. Several months before the execution of the first Saint-Lazare train station, Caillebotte painted the bridge of Europe that dominates the site as a silent witness of the technological and modern engineering progress. This grand metallic bridge, completed in 1868, is situated on the Europe Square, from which radiate six streets named after the largest cities of this continent. The metallic "X" shaped beams direct the viewer's eyes to the Saint Petersburg street.

The artist is believed to have portrayed himself as the figure in a top hat who is walking towards the viewer. The young fashionably dressed woman walking slightly behind him is most likely his friend Madam Hagen. The man's gaze seemed to be focused on a young working-class man leaning against the bridge railing. The juxtaposition of social classes and their interaction is of interest to the artist, which is evident in his numerous paintings.

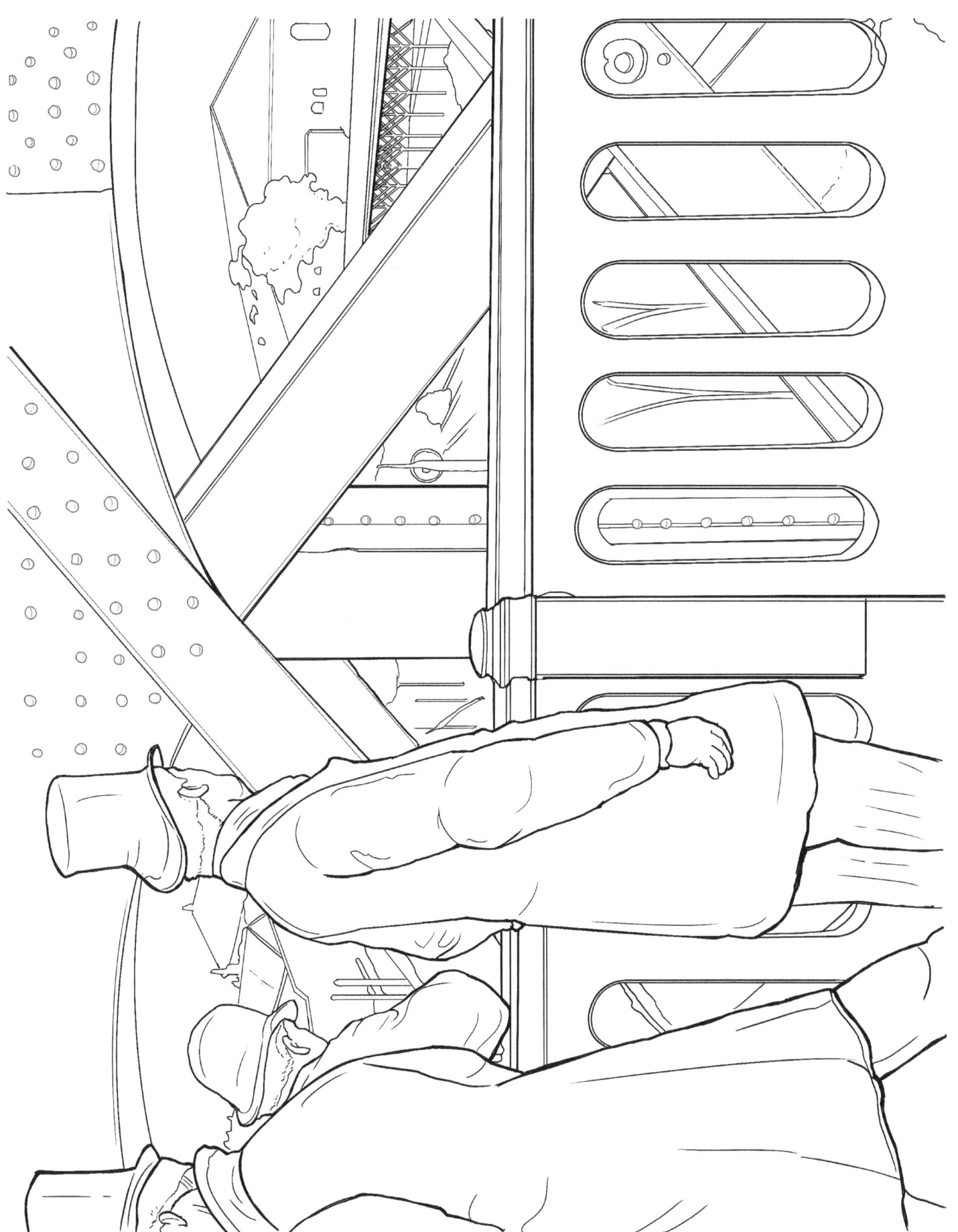

Plate 7.
On the Pont de l'Europe, **1876-77.**

In this painting Caillebotte uses monochromatic and subdued steel blue colors, which seem to reflect the cold and windy evening. The artist depicts three figures, all turned away from the viewer. The men in top hats are practically mirror images of each other, dressed in identical long coats with turned up collars. This mirror technique and the cropping of one of the figures on the far left has a photographic quality. The men dressed in a similar way also remind us of the conformed modern urban society of the 19th century, which appears to be standardized and mass-produced just as the world around them.

Caillebotte uses strong diagonals and patterns to dissect the picture into equal geometric spaces. The three figures squatter in the left half of the painting to create a sense of unbalance, as if the human figures are trying to escape the predetermined and solid symmetry of modern engineering. The men standing near the bridge railing are looking at the Saint Lazare train station, a famous subject that inspired many impressionist artists. Caillebotte's friend Monet has painted over a dozen paintings of the Saint Lazare station in 1877, three variations of which were purchased by Caillebotte for his private collection.

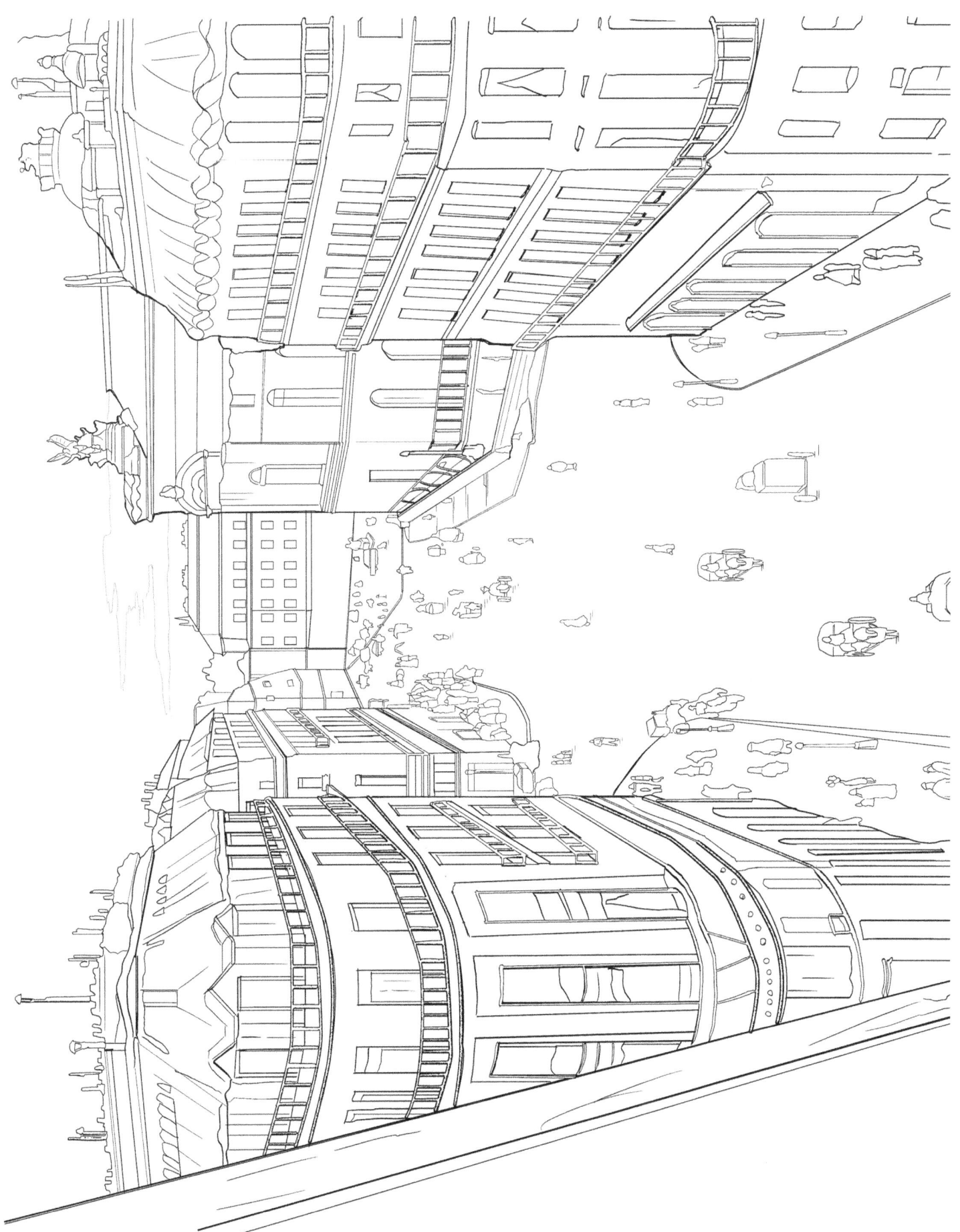

Plate 8.
Rue Halévy, Seen From the 6ᵗʰ Floor, 1878.

The painting shows a slightly vertiginous downward gaze unto a vast Haussmann Paris street, Rue Halevy, named after a musician Fromental Halévy, and situated in the 9ᵗʰ arrondissement of Paris. We can notice in the background the gold winged statues on the roofs of Palais Garnier, the famous Parisian Opera house.

Caillebotte depicts an everyday scene of the Parisian urban space from a birds eye view. This perspective is slightly dizzying to the viewer, whom the artist has placed in the first rang, and suggests certain detachment, anxiety and dispassionateness of the new urban life in a big metropolis. There are numerous people walking on the streets and carriages passing by, yet they all seem to be struggling in a disorganized motion. The blue-violet and burnt yellow colors of the tenacious and thick brushstrokes seem to add even more tension to the melancholy and nostalgia of the painting and the faceless strangers on its street.

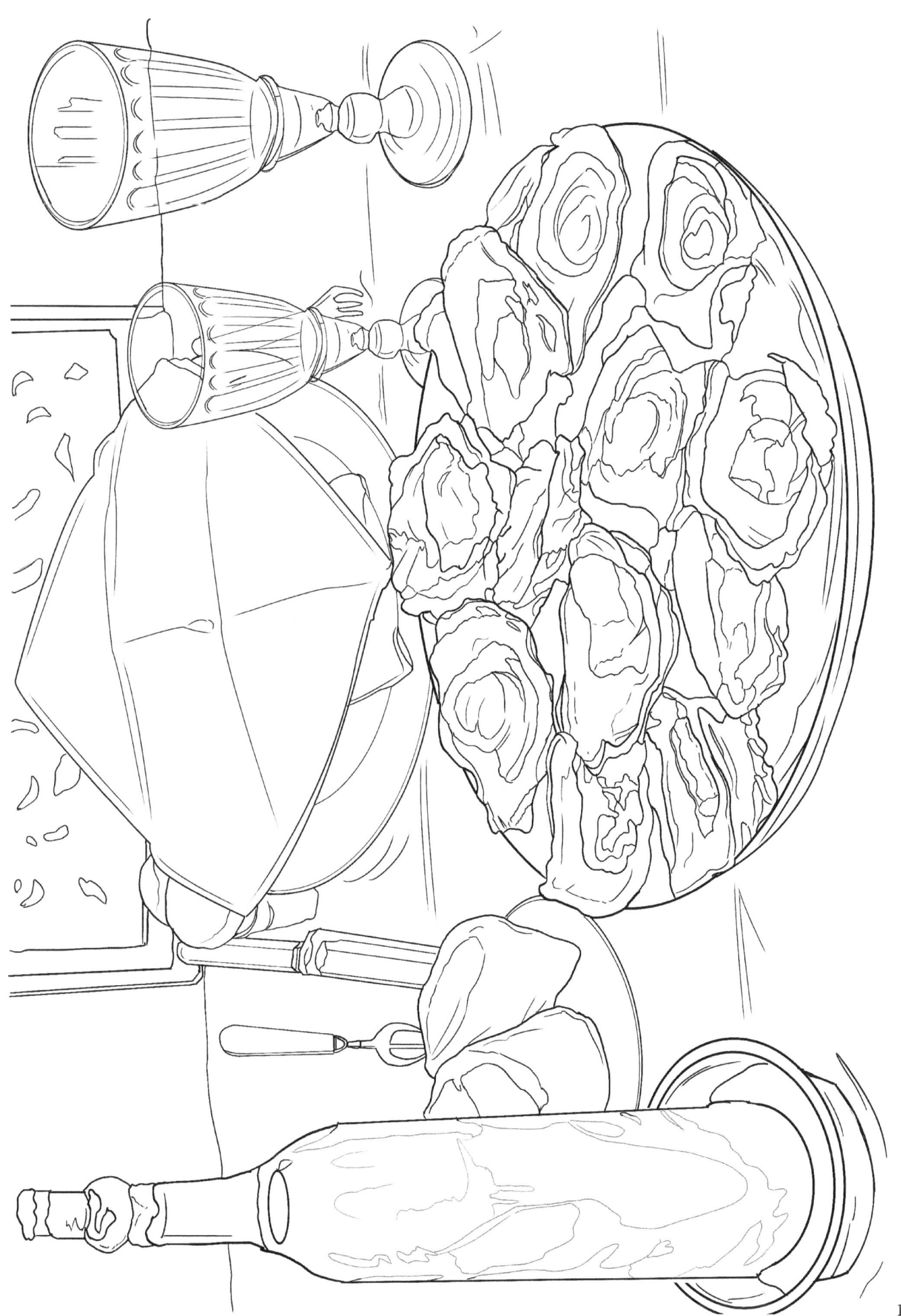

19

Plate 9.
Still Life with Oysters, **1881.**

This still life depicting oysters and lemons, perennially poised in time, is reminiscent of the realistic Dutch still life paintings of the 17th century. Oysters were traditionally a symbol of lust and appear in numerous Dutch paintings alongside carefully carved lemons and a luxurious goblet of wine. One can suggest that at the time Caillebotte mastered his still life composition techniques, he drew his inspiration from the old still life masters such as Jan van de Velde and Pieter Claesz, known for their magnificent oyster and lemons arrangements. The bottle and the wine glasses in Caillebotte's painting provide strong vertical elements that balance the horizontal rows of the oyster shells and the horizontal creases of the table cloth and the table napkin folds.

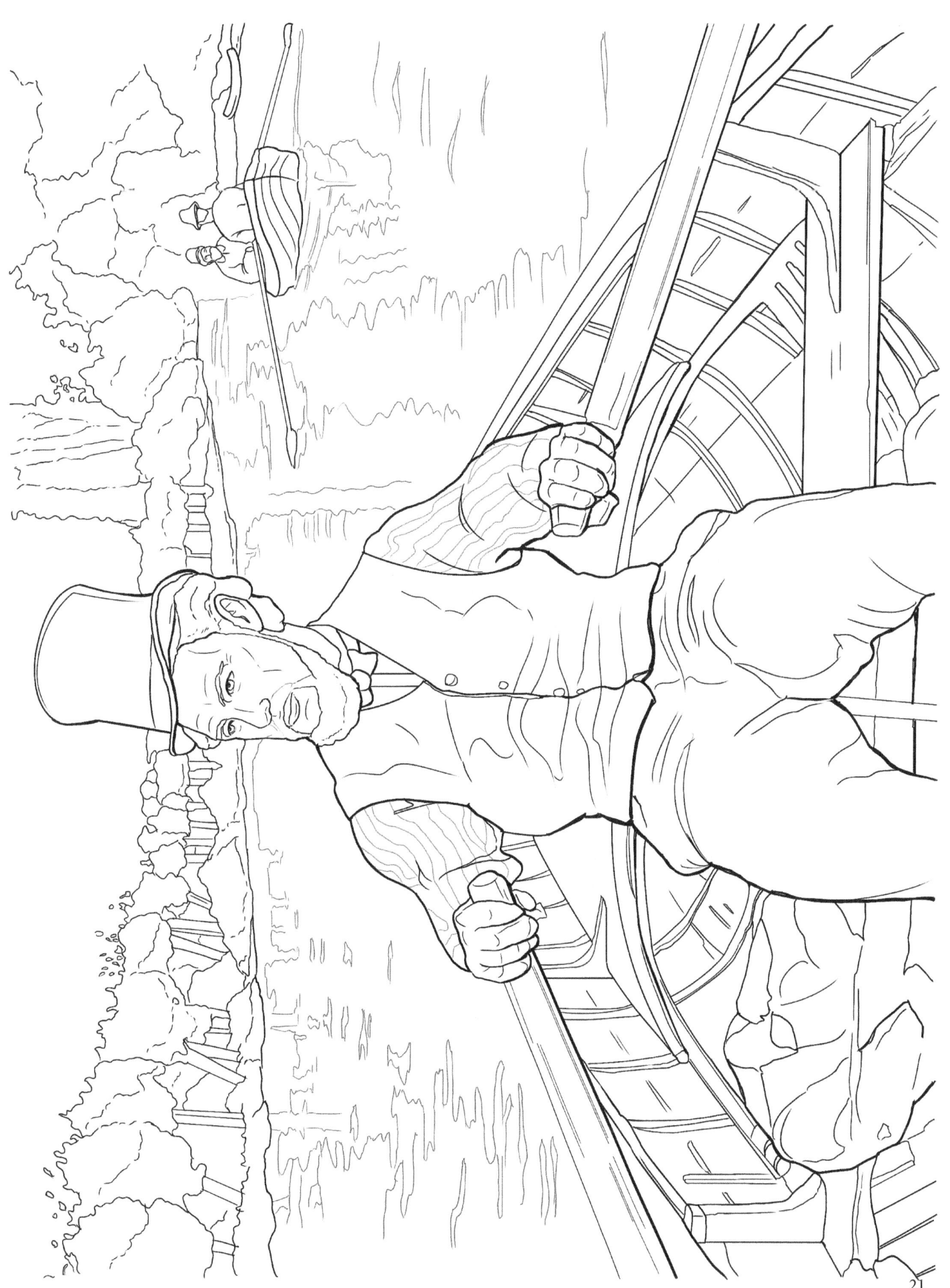

Plate 10.
Boating Party, 1877-1878.

This painting depicting a rowing man in a top hat, also known as *Oarsman in a Top Hat*, belongs to the series of seven paintings of boatmen by Caillebotte. The composition of the painting is cinematic; in the movie industry it is referred to as "the subjective camera". In this close spatial arrangement, the artist (or the spectator) becomes a part of the action, by being seated facing the figure represented in *Boating Party*. This tromp-l'oeil effect was most likely inspired by Caillebotte's avid interest in the advances of photography as an art form, and by the invention of wide-angle photographic lenses since 1860's.

The close-up perspective of the rower and the boat shows a great sense of movement. The boat is slightly tilted and man's right hand is higher than the left one, highlighting the sense of continuous motion. The man in the foreground is painted in a very detailed and realistic style, with an apparent photographic quality in his facial expression, his clothing and the details of the boat. The background and the water with green foliage reflections and bright reflections of light are executed in a more impressionistic style with fragmented loose brushwork and light colors.

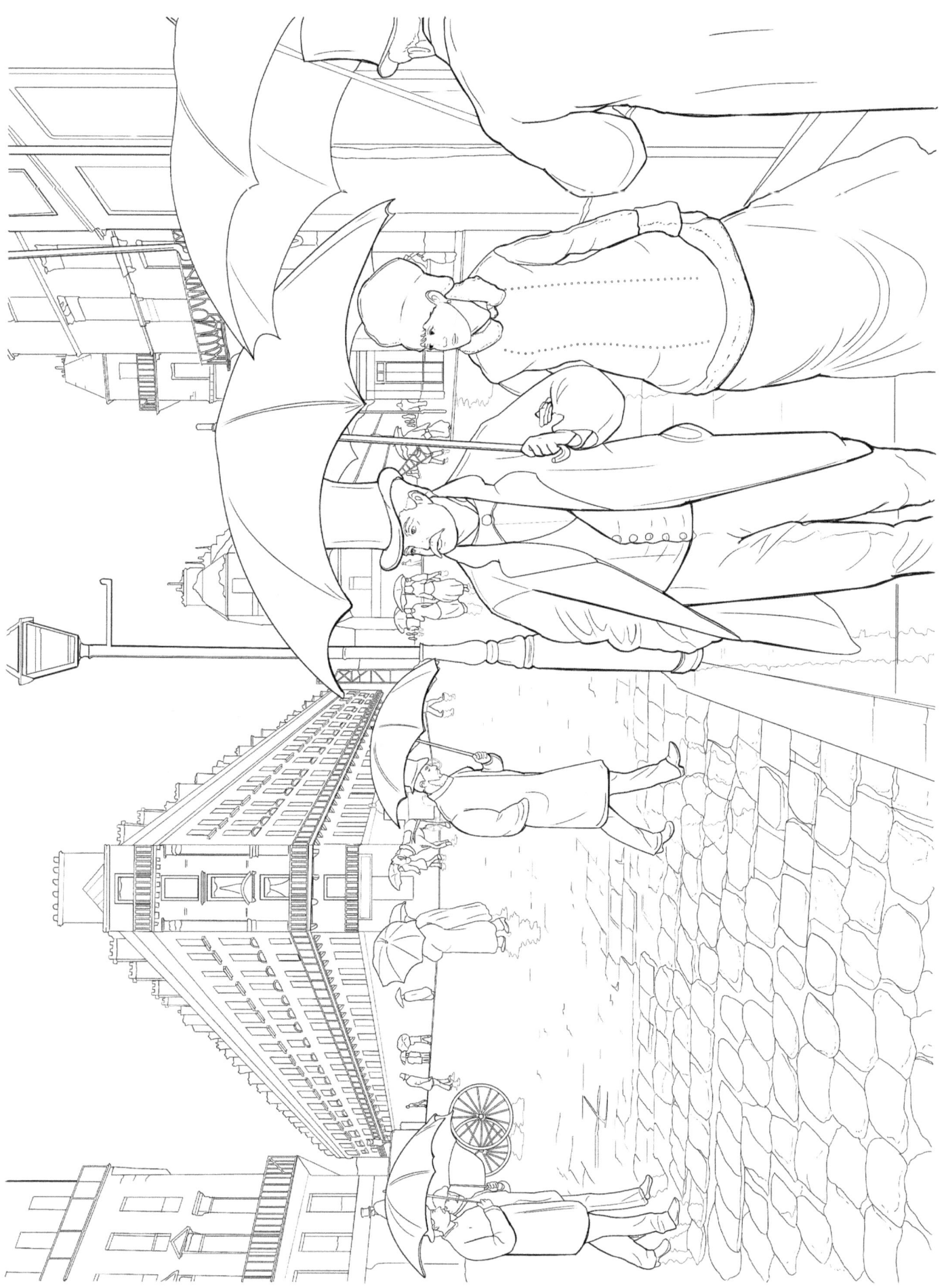

Plate 11.
Paris Street Rainy Day, 1877.

The artist is widely recognized for his realistic landscape paintings depicting urban Parisian streets and upper-class home settings of the 19th century. One of Caillebotte's most known work, "Paris Street : Rainy Day". In this work Gustave portrays a typical rainy day in the center of Paris, masterfully playing with the effects of light, shadows and wet reflections on the ground and on passer-by umbrellas. The artist uses flat and subdued pastel colors, the brushstrokes are careful, and unlike the massive brushstrokes of his fellow impressionist artists, we can see vivid lines and contours. Yet the overall feeling is light and effervescent.

The scene is very modern, showing wide and vast boulevards and new apartment buildings in Haussmann style. This was the era of Haussmann's renovation of Paris, when numerous medieval crowded neighborhoods were demolished and in its place rose the vast new squares and wide networks of boulevards. The painting depicts an intersection close to the Saint Lazare station. One may say the painting is also an intersection of social classes, which was a very modern and controversial theme at the time. In the foreground we see three upper-class figures who are very elegantly and fashionably dressed. The man on the right is cut off, a new technique reminiscent of the cropped photographs. In the background we can notice little figures belonging to a lower Parisian social class, those of a painter holding a ladder and a *bonne de chambre* opening up her umbrella.

www.ingramcontent.com/pod-product-compliance
Lightning Source LLC
Chambersburg PA
CBHW081249170526

45165CB00009B/3252